ALL THE BEST POTATOES

Cookbooks by Joie Warner
ALL THE BEST PASTA SAUCES
ALL THE BEST SALADS
ALL THE BEST PIZZAS
ALL THE BEST CHICKEN DINNERS
ALL THE BEST MEXICAN MEALS
ALL THE BEST MUFFINS AND QUICK BREADS
ALL THE BEST POTATOES
ALL THE BEST COOKIES
ALL THE BEST PASTA SAUCES II
ALL THE BEST RICE
THE COMPLETE BOOK OF CHICKEN WINGS
THE BRAUN HAND BLENDER COOKBOOK
A TASTE OF CHINATOWN
JOIE WARNER'S SPAGHETTI
JOIE WARNER'S CAESAR SALADS
JOIE WARNER'S APPLE DESERTS

ALL THE BEST

POTATOES

BY
JOIE WARNER

A FLAVOR BOOK

Published in Canada by

Stoddart Publishing Co. Limited
34 Lesmill Road
Don Mills, Ontario M3B 2T6

CANADIAN CATALOGING IN PUBLICATION DATA
Warner, Joie.
     All the best potatoes
Includes index.
ISBN 0-7737-5629-9
1. Cookery (Potatoes).   2. Potatoes.   I. Title.
TX803.P8W37   1994   641.6'521   C93-095342-8

Printed in the United States of America
10 9 8 7 6 5 4 3 2 1

This book was created and produced by

Flavor Publications, Inc.
208 East 51st Street, Suite 240
New York, New York 10022

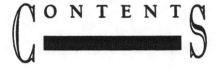

CONTENTS

INTRODUCTION

THE ONCE HUMBLE POTATO is enjoying a phenomenal renaissance. This nutrient-packed, low-calorie, fiber-rich vegetable now has a long-deserved starring role on today's dinner plate. Our new-found fascination with potatoes is coming about in part because potato proponents have finally got the message out: potatoes are not fattening – they're virtually fat free! The truth is, a medium-sized steamed, baked, or boiled potato without the addition of butter has only about 100 calories. Add butter and milk to those mashed potatoes and the calories climb to about 250; deep-fry that same potato and the calories soar to nearly 450! Let's get this straight: it's the butter, milk, and sour cream that are villains – not the poor potato!

The fact is, potatoes are the perfect diet food. Good news for those watching their waistline – you can dine on these delectable tubers with a clear conscience. Nutritionally, potatoes are a rich source of protein, minerals, such as iron and potassium, vitamin C, as well as vitamins A, B1, and B6. They contain complex carbohydrates (the good kind), and are quite filling, leaving one happily satisfied. Now that doesn't mean you have to give up butter altogether, unless of course, that's what your doctor says. I happen to subscribe to the notion that you can eat whatever you want – butter, cream, et al – in moderation or occasionally. Personally, I believe it's all right to eat french fries as long as they're homemade. Not only do they taste better and fresher, they contain more nutrients, too. And since deep-frying is a bit of a bother, a serving of french fries becomes a rare treat. (I have included recipes for both deep-fried and oven-baked french fries. I highly recommend the oven-baked ones – they are so healthy, I call them the eat-as-many-as-you-want variety!)

Another reason for the spud's resurgence in popularity is that many gourmet vegetable stores and supermarkets now offer potatoes in a wondrous rainbow of colors: from purple to pink, red to blue, yellow to jet black. Plus cooks and chefs everywhere are discovering mind-boggling ways to prepare potatoes, from good old-fashioned hash browns to haute dishes dressed in inventive new ways.

The versatile spud can be boiled, broiled, steamed, sautéed, deep-fried, mashed, roasted, baked, ground into flour – you name it. From the first to the last meal of the day, potatoes get served up as appetizers and snacks, soups and stews, salads and sides dishes, condiments, breads, omelets, dumplings, stuffings, pastas and pancakes – and even desserts.

While today the potato is the world's leading vegetable crop, it wasn't always so. In times gone past, potatoes were thought evil and blamed for every ailment under the sun. People around the world refused to eat this "deadly" member of the nightshade family.

It was the Spanish conquistadors who discovered potatoes while stealing the Inca's gold and brought them back to Europe in 1534. The Incas had been cultivating and worshiping the potato (some 4,000 varieties!) since about 3000 B.C. The Andean people have given the tuber regal status because of its sustaining powers and still worship it today.

In America, potatoes account for more than one-third of all vegetables consumed, and potato chips are the leading salted snack food. Let's face it, to many people there are only two ways to eat potatoes – chips or fries – though baked potatoes are apparently challenging french fries for the number one spot. To others, the spud in the form of mashed potatoes is the perfect comfort food.

Much as I adore mashed potatoes and french fries, my potato repertoire includes a much wider range of dishes. While most are American classics, many are inspired by other cuisines. *All the Best Potatoes* is a collection of my favorite potato recipes – all of them fast and easy to cook. Here you'll find dishes to fit any fancy, from a casual breakfast or picnic to an elegant dinner or a comforting midnight snack.

Chapter One includes appetizers and snacks – classics like potato skins – and sophisticated appetizers, too, such as Little Potato Nests with Smoked Salmon and Caviar. Soups range from Potato and Leek with Stilton to comforting Clam and Potato Chowder. The salad chapter includes plenty of potato salads from the homey to the unusual, with ingredients such as sun-dried tomatoes and mint, or blue cheese and pecans. The main courses include recipes for Greek Chicken and Potatoes, wonderful air-light Potato Gnocchi with Two Sauces (Tomato Basil and Creamy Gorgonzola), and Seafood Potato Pie. You'll also find recipes for fried and sautéed potatoes; mashed and baked potatoes; breads and rolls, and the last chapter is dedicated to scrumptious desserts like Sweet Potato Pie in Chocolate Crumb Crust. There's also a glossary of ingredients and basics covering different types of potatoes, plus advice on buying and storing.

My eclectic assortment is the result of my penchant – or is it a passion – for potatoes. I do hope you'll discover some fresh ideas, as well as some time-honored favorites, to add to your own repertoire.

JOIE WARNER

♦ ♦ ♦

BASICS

POTATO VARIETIES

There are hundreds of potato species with a wide range of colors, flavors, and shapes, but most potatoes fall into two types: starchy (mealy) and dry fleshed, or waxy and firm textured.

RUSSET OR IDAHO POTATO: This large, oblong, brown-skinned potato has a satisfying fluffy-textured interior when cooked, making it perfect for baked and mashed potatoes, french fries, home fries, dumplings, gratins, soups, and for thickening other dishes. (While most people assume firm-fleshed, waxy red potatoes are the only type of potato for salads, I beg to differ. I personally relish the russet's or Idaho's starchy quality in potato salads, too.)

YUKON GOLD POTATO: A yellow-fleshed, medium-starch potato created in Canada, it can be used interchangeably with other varieties whether baked, boiled, steamed, mashed, or fried.

ROUND RED POTATO: Round, red potatoes with thin skins ranging in color from pink to ruby red, are often labeled "new" or "boiling" potatoes. This firm, waxy-textured spud doesn't fall apart when boiled – the ideal potato for steaming, roasting, and boiling – any dish, like a salad, where potatoes need to keep their shape.

ROUND WHITE POTATO: An all-purpose potato with light-colored, thin skin, it, too, is often labeled "new". This low-starch potato is quite similar to the red potato in taste and texture, making it excellent for boiling and sautéing.

NEW POTATOES: Not a special variety, new potatoes are actually immature potatoes (starchy or waxy) that are freshly dug and have never been stored. The smallest new potatoes – marble-size "pee wees" – are exquisite either boiled or steamed, served with just a drizzle of butter and perhaps a sprinkling of fresh herbs.

SWEET POTATO: Often erroneously labeled "yams" (a yam is another vegetable altogether), it's so named to denote a type of sweet potato that is sweeter, deeper-colored, and moister than the paler variety. And if that's not confusing enough, the sweet potato is technically not a potato either. (But not to worry, "yams" and sweet potatoes are interchangeable in any recipe.) Sweet potatoes belong to the morning glory family, potatoes to the nightshade family. Oblong and irregularly shaped, sweet-potato flesh ranges from pinkish-orange to deep orange. I prefer the moister, deep-orange variety (the one often labeled a yam). Sweet potatoes contain more minerals, vitamin A and C than white potatoes, as well as slightly more calories. They are very versatile, too: they take beautifully to baking, mashing, and puréeing and are often found in desserts such as puddings and pies.

EXOTIC VARIETIES: Potato devotees can now find unusual varieties, such as the blue Peruvian, in specialty produce stores and farmers' markets. Best enjoyed steamed or boiled, they can be combined with other potatoes for a colorful effect or simply drizzled with butter and snippets of fresh herbs. If you come upon other "exotic" varieties such as fingerlings and the Caribe, consult your greengrocer, the potato marketing board, or seed catalogs for cooking and serving suggestions.

THE STARCH TEST

If you are confused as to whether your potato is of the starchy or the waxy type, here's a simple test from Harold McGee's *On Food and Cooking*: Make a brine of 2 parts water to 1 part salt. Add your potato. If it floats, it's waxy; if it sinks, it's starchy.

CHOOSING POTATOES

Select potatoes with smooth, unblemished skins and avoid any that are discolored, moldy, or have begun to sprout – indicating they've been hanging around far too long. Potatoes shouldn't be bruised, soft, or have green-tinged skins – signaling the presence of the toxin solanine which develops when potatoes are exposed to light. Cut away any green parts before cooking – the toxins could make you ill and they impart a bitter taste. Spurn potatoes with sprouting eyes, for they are well past their prime. But if you do choose to use potatoes that are sprouting, be sure to cut out the sprouts before cooking: they contain a toxin that can be harmful if eaten.

HOW TO STORE POTATOES

Always remove potatoes from their plastic bags as soon as you get them home or they'll become moldy very quickly. Don't store potatoes in a warm place – they'll begin to soften, shrivel, and sprout within days. Also, storing potatoes with onions or garlic hastens mold. Potatoes keep longest in a cool, dark, dry place, between 45° to 50°F – never in the refrigerator where the starch will convert to sugar, giving them a funny, sweet taste. (Potatoes don't freeze either: they turn watery.) They are best stored in a vegetable bin or on a rack with good air circulation. Never wash potatoes before storing or they will quickly decay.

TO PEEL OR NOT TO PEEL

We all know that potato skins contain fiber, so of course it's best never to peel them before cooking. These days, I prefer not to peel potatoes when making french fries – not because I'm lazy or particularly health conscious – I just simply love the texture and appearance with the skin on. Don't peel your potatoes until just prior to cooking or they'll discolor – unless the recipe specifies otherwise – and then they'll be soaked in a water solution. It's also preferable not to peel potatoes before boiling them to prevent loss of vitamins, but when I'm in a hurry, peeling first does save time. Try to peel away as little of the flesh as possible, but don't worry too much – there's plenty of nutrients left.

INGREDIENTS

ANCHOVIES: My recipes use the canned anchovy fillets in oil. Some brands are saltier than others, so experiment until you find a brand you like.

BASIL: Most supermarkets and greengrocers now offer fresh herbs. In any recipe calling for fresh basil, do not substitute dried.

BLACK OLIVES: I use Kalamata olives from Greece in my recipes. You may also use Niçoise olives from France. They are available in specialty food shops and many supermarkets. Canned American olives do not have the flavor or pungency needed for the recipes in this book.

BLACK PEPPER: I always use freshly ground black peppercorns.

CAMBOZOLA: A creamy-textured, mild blue cheese from Germany.

CAPERS: These are the unopened flower buds of a Mediterranean shrub. Tiny French capers are used in the following recipes. They are packed in vinegar (not salt), and I never rinse them.

CHEDDAR CHEESE: Use best-quality, extra-sharp Cheddar cheese for the recipes in this book.

CHICKEN STOCK: Homemade is best, but canned is perfectly acceptable. Do not use chicken bouillon cubes.

CHICKPEAS: A variety of legumes also called garbanzos. The canned variety is used in these recipes.

CHILES: Jars and cans of pickled sliced jalapeños are available in most supermarkets in the Mexican food section.

COCONUT MILK: This is the liquid obtained from pressing the coconut flesh, not the liquid found inside the coconut. I use the unsweetened canned coconut milk (not the sweetened coconut cream for drinks). The best coconut milk comes from Thailand. The brand I use has a picture of a measuring cup and a coconut on the label. It's available in Asian food stores.

CORIANDER: A pungently aromatic herb also known as cilantro or Chinese parsley. It's available in Asian and Latin American food shops, some supermarkets, and produce stores.

CREAM: Heavy or whipping cream contains at least 35% butterfat. Light cream contains 18 to 20% and is therefore lower in calories and does not whip or thicken.

CREAM CHEESE: For best flavor, purchase a good quality cream cheese – preferably one freshly made by a local dairy or cheesemaker. It's available in most cheese shops, supermarkets, and specialty food shops. Recipes specify cream cheese to be at room temperature so that it is softened enough to blend easily.

DRIED HERBS: The fresher the dried herbs, the more flavorful your food. Bottled herbs that have lost their color and aroma should be replaced.

FETA CHEESE: This tangy Greek cheese – both domestic and imported – is available in most cheese shops, supermarkets, and specialty food shops.

GARLIC: It is hard to imagine anyone not cooking with garlic (lots of it!), for it is a seasoning that goes with almost every savory dish and besides, garlic is good for you. Choose large bulbs that are tightly closed and not sprouting. Squeeze the bulb to make sure it is firm and fresh. Powdered garlic should be avoided in any recipe calling for fresh garlic though it is perfectly acceptable when used with other dried herbs in seasoning mixes for "dry" marinades.

GINGER: Always use fresh ginger unless otherwise specified. Powdered ginger and fresh ginger aren't interchangeable. Select young ginger with smooth, shiny skin. Ginger lasts for months in the refrigerator if first wrapped in a paper towel, then placed in a plastic bag. The paper towel must be replaced often: it will become moldy otherwise.

GOAT CHEESE: For the recipes in this book, I use the fresh, soft, mild-tasting variety. Goat cheese is available at most supermarkets and cheese shops.

GORGONZOLA: A very creamy, mold-ripened cheese from the Lombardy region of Italy. Its delicate, sharp flavor is wonderful. It's available in Italian food shops, well-stocked cheese stores, and supermarkets.

JALAPEÑOS: I use the canned pickled or brine-packed variety in the recipes in this book. They are available at most supermarkets in the Mexican food section.

LEEKS: To clean, slice leek in half lengthwise, leaving root intact. Place under cold, running water, fanning the sections as necessary to remove sand. Drain well.

NUTMEG: Purchase whole nutmegs and grate them just before using for best flavor.

OLIVE OIL: I prefer good-quality olive oil with a delicate olive taste for cooking. Try different brands because price doesn't always equate with quality.

PARMESAN: Be sure to purchase Parmesan that has the words "Parmigiano Reggiano" or second best, "Grana Padano" stamped on the rind. Always grate it fresh just before using: it begins to lose flavor after grating. It is available in Italian food shops or well-stocked cheese stores.

PARSLEY: I prefer the flat-leaf variety which is available in most supermarkets and quality greengrocers.

ROMANO CHEESE: Pecorino Romano is a grating cheese similar to Parmesan cheese, but with a sharper flavor. Like Parmesan, it is best freshly grated.

SALMON ROE: Salmon caviar is available at quality fish shops and some supermarkets. It is very perishable and should be bought frozen or just thawed and used as soon as possible.

STILTON CHEESE: A delicious blue cheese from Britain.

SUN-DRIED TOMATOES: Salty, with an intense flavor of tomatoes, the best ones are imported from Italy – though there are some quality domestic varieties. Sun-dried tomatoes are available in most specialty and Italian food stores. They are available dry-packed or in oil, in jars. Dry-packed should be aromatic and somewhat pliable – not hard and brown – and reddish colored. Before use, place dry-packed tomatoes in a footed strainer and pour boiling water over to soften them. Pack in sterilized jars and cover with olive oil. You may also add a garlic clove, some oregano, and black peppercorns for added flavor. Store in the refrigerator, but bring back to room temperature before using.

TOMATOES, CANNED: Buy the best Italian or domestic brands available (experiment until you find a brand you like), for it makes an enormous difference in the taste and quality of sauces. Crush them in your hands as you add them to your sauce or crush them in the skillet with a wooden spoon if you don't like getting your hands messy.

TOMATOES, FRESH: In the summer I cook with fresh, ripe, unwaxed, regular tomatoes. At other times of the year, I purchase cherry or plum tomatoes which, if left at room temperature to ripen, have more flavor than out-of-season tomatoes. Always leave them at room temperature for best flavor; don't refrigerate unless they begin to overripen.

VERMOUTH: I use dry white French vermouth in my recipes instead of dry white wine. You may substitute dry white wine, of course.

WHITE KIDNEY BEANS: Also known as cannellini beans. I use the canned variety in these recipes. They are usually drained in a colander and gently rinsed under cold water to remove the thick brine. Purchase a good brand – the beans should be whole and not mushy.

ZEST: The colored outer layer of skin on a citrus fruit. Use only the colored portion because the white part is bitter.

◆ ◆ ◆

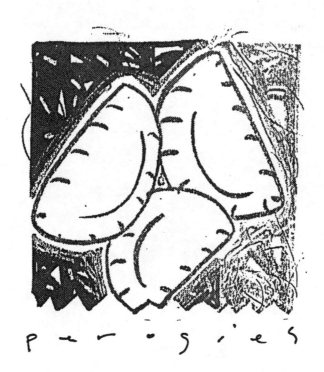

perogies

APPETIZERS & SNACKS

◆ ◆ ◆

Typically served as an accompaniment to fried fish or fried vegetables such as eggplant, _scordalia_ is also served with warm pita bread. ◆ This is _very_ generously flavored with garlic – if you love _hummus_ (garlicky chickpea dip) or _tzatziki_ (garlicky yogurt), then you'll enjoy this unusual dish.

GREEK POTATO AND GARLIC DIP

4 large garlic cloves
2 cups warm unseasoned
   mashed potatoes
   (2 large russets)
1 cup olive oil
¼ cup fresh lemon juice
Salt

Freshly ground black
   pepper
⅓ cup fresh flat-leaf parsley
Greek black olives
   (Kalamata)
Pita bread, warmed in oven
   and cut into triangles

FINELY CHOP GARLIC in food processor. Add potatoes, ½ cup olive oil, lemon juice, salt, and pepper; process until very smooth. With machine running, add remaining oil in thin stream and continue processing until the consistency of mayonnaise. Add parsley and process until chopped. Taste and adjust seasoning. Serve a generous dollop on a plate accompanied by olives and warm pita bread. Makes about 1½ cups.

OVEN-CRISPED POTATO SKINS WITH BACON, ONION, AND SOUR CREAM

2 pounds (4 large) russet
   potatoes, scrubbed
5 bacon slices, diced
2 tablespoons melted butter
Salt

Freshly ground black
   pepper
About ¼ cup sour cream
1 large whole green onion,
   finely chopped

PREHEAT OVEN to 425°F.

Bake potatoes for 1 hour or until tender. Remove from oven, allow to cool enough to handle, cut in half, and scoop out most of the potato flesh leaving ¼-inch thick shell (reserve potato flesh for another use).

Meanwhile, cook bacon in small skillet until crisp; remove with slotted spoon to paper towel-lined plate to drain.

Turn oven heat up to 450°F. Brush both sides of potato skins with butter and place on baking sheet. Sprinkle with salt and pepper. Bake for 12 minutes or until crisp. Remove from oven, dollop each shell with sour cream, sprinkle with green onion and bacon bits. Serves 2.

B*acon, green onion, and sour cream are perfect partners for potato skins. ◆ An upscale variation: substitute caviar for the bacon.*

Spud skins – popular restaurant fare – are fun and easy to make at home. ◆ This recipe can be doubled or tripled.

OVEN-CRISPED TEX-MEX POTATO SKINS

1 pound (2 large) russet potatoes, scrubbed
2 tablespoons melted butter
Salt
Freshly ground black pepper
6 ounces grated sharp Cheddar cheese

2 tablespoons coarsely chopped pickled sliced jalapeños
1 whole green onion, chopped
2 tablespoons coarsely chopped fresh coriander
Sour cream for serving

PREHEAT OVEN to 425°F.

Bake potatoes for 1 hour or until tender. Remove from oven, allow to cool enough to handle, cut in half, and scoop out most of the potato flesh leaving ¼-inch thick shell (reserve potato flesh for another use).

Turn oven heat up to 450°F. Brush both sides of potato skins with butter and place on baking sheet. Sprinkle with salt and pepper. Bake for 12 minutes or until crisp. Remove from oven, fill shells with cheese, chiles, and green onion and place under broiler for 2 minutes or until cheese is bubbly. Remove from oven, sprinkle with coriander, and serve with sour cream. Serves 2.

POTATO LATKES WITH SOUR CREAM AND APPLESAUCE

1 medium-large onion
2 pounds (4 large) russet or
  Yukon Gold potatoes,
  peeled
1 large egg
2 tablespoons all-purpose
  flour

1½ teaspoons salt
Freshly ground black
  pepper
About ¼ cup vegetable oil
Sour cream for serving
Applesauce for serving

USING LARGEST OPENINGS of a 4-sided grater, or large openings of food processor grater, first grate onion, then potatoes into large bowl and immediately combine to prevent potatoes from discoloring. Transfer mixture to colander and using hands, squeeze out as much liquid as possible, then place in clean, dry bowl. Stir in egg, flour, salt, and pepper until thoroughly combined.

Heat about ¼ cup oil in large nonstick skillet over medium-high heat. Drop about a scant ¼ cup potato mixture per pancake, about 4 at a time, into hot oil – flattening each one slightly with back of spoon – and cook for 3 minutes each side or until golden brown and crisp. Transfer to paper-towel-lined plate to drain. Repeat with remaining potato mixture, adding more oil as needed. Serve immediately with plenty of sour cream and applesauce. Makes about 14 pancakes.

These delectable potato pancakes – a Jewish specialty traditionally eaten at Hanukkah – are delicious served at any time of the year as snacks or appetizers, for lunch, or even as a light dinner. ◆ Wonderful served with both sour cream and applesauce, they become quite the treat when topped with sour cream and golden caviar and/or smoked salmon. ◆ Latkes are best eaten freshly made, but you may freeze cooked latkes on a baking sheet; when solid, place in a freezer bag and store for up to 2 weeks. Partially thaw and reheat in 450°F oven for about 6 minutes or until very hot.

Polish-style potato-stuffed dumplings make a delightful first course, light lunch, or snack. They're also great do-ahead fare: easily prepared and frozen days or weeks in advance. ♦ I've cheated time and trouble by using pre-made Chinese dumpling wrappers in place of homemade perogi dumplings. Purchase the thickish, white-colored, 3-inch round wrappers used for the <u>dim sum</u> dumplings called <u>pot stickers</u> – not won ton wrappers. They're sold fresh in packages, usually beside the fresh noodles at Asian grocers labeled either "dumpling wrappers" or "gyoza".

EASY POTATO AND CHEESE PEROGIES

3 cups warm unseasoned
   mashed potatoes
   (3 large russets)
8 ounces grated extra-sharp
   Cheddar cheese
1 large whole green onion,
   finely chopped
1½ teaspoons salt
½ teaspoon freshly ground
   black pepper

1 package dumpling
   wrappers
Butter for drizzling
Sour cream for serving
Chopped green onion
   (green part only)
   for serving

THOROUGHLY BLEND POTATOES, cheese, green onion, salt, and pepper in large bowl.

Place about 1 tablespoon filling in center of each dumpling wrapper, dampen edges with a little water, and fold over circles into half-moon shapes. Seal by pressing closed with your fingers, then go around edges with tines of a fork to make a pattern and seal tightly. At this point, you may place the dumplings in one layer on foil-lined tray and freeze; when solid, place in freezer bag.

To cook, drop about 4 to 6 dumplings per serving into large pot of salted boiling water and cook for 4 minutes or until dough is cooked and filling heated through. Drain well; place on warmed plates. Heat about 3 tablespoons butter per serving in small skillet and cook until it begins to brown. Drizzle over perogies and garnish with a dollop of sour cream and chopped green onions. Pass the peppermill and extra sour cream at the table. Makes about 40 dumplings.

LITTLE POTATO NESTS WITH SMOKED SALMON AND CAVIAR

1 pound (2 large) russet potatoes, peeled
1 large egg
2 tablespoons all-purpose flour
½ teaspoon salt
About 3 cups vegetable oil

16 generous teaspoons sour cream
About 1 ounce best-quality, thinly-sliced smoked salmon, cut into bite-size pieces
5 ounces fresh salmon roe

GRATE POTATOES using largest openings of a 4-sided grater, or large openings of food processor grater. Using hands, squeeze out as much liquid as possible, then place in medium bowl. Stir in egg, flour, and salt until thoroughly combined.

Pour enough oil to cover the strainer into heavy medium saucepan or deep-fryer and heat oil to 360°F.

Meanwhile, divide the potato mixture into 16 portions. Coat strainer with vegetable spray. Gently press potato mixture into strainer to shape a nest. Immerse nest in strainer in hot oil, cook for 1 to 2 minutes or until nest is completely crisp and golden brown. Carefully remove nest with spoon and place on newspaper or brown paper grocery bag to drain. Continue with remaining potato mixture. (If nests aren't completely crisp, just return them to hot oil without strainer for a few seconds or until crisp.)

Just before serving, fill each nest with a dollop of sour cream, 2 or more pieces of salmon, and top with a dollop of salmon roe. Serve at once. Makes 16 nests.

G*orgeous mouthfuls of crispy-fried shredded potato topped with sour cream, smoked salmon, and salmon caviar. Enjoy these oh-so-chic hors d'oeuvres with some "bubbly" or cocktails. ♦ You'll need one or more small metal strainers — about 2-inches in diameter — to shape the nests. ♦ You can fry the nests a few hours ahead and leave them, uncovered, at room temperature until filling.*

saucepan

S O U P S

♦ ♦ ♦

C

hilly-day soup – a country-
style combination of smoked
kielbasa sausage, white
kidney beans, potatoes, and

spinach.

SMOKED SAUSAGE SOUP
WITH POTATOES AND GREENS

1 tablespoon olive oil
1 large onion, chopped
½ pound smoked kielbasa
    sausage, casing removed,
    thinly sliced, then
    quartered
5 cups water
19-ounce can white kidney
    beans, drained
¾ pound (2 medium)
    russet potatoes, peeled
    and cubed

2 cups fresh spinach leaves,
    coarsely chopped
½ teaspoon salt
Freshly ground black
    pepper
1 tablespoon red wine
    vinegar

HEAT OIL in large heavy saucepan over medium-high heat.
Add onion and cook for 2 minutes or until tender. Add
sausage and cook 3 minutes or until it begins to brown. Add
water, kidney beans, and potatoes and bring to a boil.
Reduce heat and simmer for 20 minutes or until potatoes
are tender.

    Just before serving, add spinach, salt, pepper, and vine-
gar. Pass the peppermill at the table. Serves 6.

POTATO AND PASTA SOUP
WITH BASIL AND MINT

6 cups water
2 teaspoons salt
1 cup elbow macaroni
1 large onion, chopped
4 large garlic cloves,
  chopped
2 pounds (4 large) russet or
  white potatoes, peeled
  and cubed
1 generous tablespoon
  butter

1 cup coarsely shredded
  fresh basil leaves
½ cup coarsely chopped
  fresh mint leaves
Freshly ground black
  pepper
¼ cup freshly grated
  Romano or Parmesan
  cheese plus extra for
  serving

BRING WATER TO A BOIL in large heavy saucepan. Stir in salt; add macaroni and cook, stirring occasionally, for 4 minutes. Reduce heat to medium, add onion, garlic, and potatoes; simmer for 10 minutes or until potatoes and onion are tender. Stir in butter, basil, mint, pepper, and Romano cheese. Serve at once accompanied by extra grated cheese. Serves 6 to 8.

This "peasant" soup is simplicity itself, consisting primarily of water, pasta, onions, garlic, potatoes, and a bounty of fresh herbs. ◆ The soup must be served the minute it's prepared, and the herbs added at the moment just before serving.

A pretty pale orange soup with a delicate flavor. ♦ I've cut the sweetness – I find many sweet potato soups too cloying – by using half sweet potato and half white potato.

SWEET POTATO SOUP

2 tablespoons butter
1 large onion, chopped
1 pound (3 medium) sweet
   potatoes, peeled and
   cubed
1 pound (2 large) russet
   potatoes, peeled and
   cubed

5 cups chicken stock
⅓ cup heavy cream
½ teaspoon ground ginger
1 teaspoon salt
Freshly ground white or
   black pepper

MELT BUTTER in large heavy saucepan over medium-high heat. Add onion and cook 2 minutes or until tender. Add potatoes and chicken stock and bring to a boil. Reduce heat, partially cover, and simmer for 1 hour or until potatoes are very tender.

Pureé in batches in food processor or blender and return to saucepan. Add cream, ginger, salt, and pepper; simmer for 5 minutes to blend flavors. Pass the peppermill at the table. Serves 4.

POTATO AND LEEK SOUP
WITH STILTON

3 tablespoons butter
2 cups chopped white and
    pale-green part leeks
    (previously well rinsed)
1½ pounds (3 large) russet
    potatoes, peeled and
    cubed
5 cups chicken stock

1½ teaspoons salt
Freshly ground white
    pepper
½ cup heavy cream
4 ounces crumbled Stilton
    cheese, at room
    temperature

MELT BUTTER in large heavy saucepan over medium heat. Add leeks and cook for 5 minutes or until tender but not browned. Add potatoes, chicken stock, salt, and pepper and bring to a boil. Reduce heat to medium-low, cover, and simmer for 20 minutes or until potatoes are tender.

Pureé mixture in batches in food processor and return to saucepan. Add cream and heat through. Ladle into warmed wide shallow soup bowls and sprinkle with crumbled cheese. Serves 6.

The affinity of leeks and potatoes is showcased in this exquisite, creamy soup. ◆ *The garnish of blue cheese is not a strong presence, yet it takes the soup from simply sensational to sublime.* ◆ *Feel free to substitute any blue cheese for the Stilton.*

A bowlful of this lightly creamy soup, chock-full of fresh little-neck clams (canned clams are all right, too), potatoes, smoky bacon, and herbs is creature comfort on a dreary day. ◆ Serve with oyster crackers, if desired.

CLAM AND POTATO CHOWDER

4 pounds littleneck clams or 1 can (5-ounce) baby clams, drained, reserving ½ cup broth
1 cup water
2 cups peeled, diced russet or Yukon gold potatoes
2 tablespoons butter
2 slices bacon, diced
1 medium onion, chopped
1 cup potato water from drained cooked potatoes

1 small bay leaf
¾ teaspoon dried tarragon
½ teaspoon dried thyme
¼ teaspoon ground savory
½ teaspoon salt
½ teaspoon freshly ground black pepper
¾ cup heavy cream
Butter for garnish

RINSE CLAMS WELL under cold running water; place in large saucepan and add 1 cup water. Cover tightly; bring to a boil over high heat. Steam for 3 minutes or until clams have opened; remove from heat. Drain clams, reserving broth and discarding any unopened clams. Remove clam meat from shells, coarsely chop, and place in small bowl. Strain clam liquid through coffee filter into a bowl, then pour ½ cup into bowl containing clams, discarding remaining liquid.

Alternately, set aside canned clams with ½ cup broth.

Boil potatoes in water to cover just until tender, about 3 minutes; drain, reserving potato liquid. Set aside.

In heavy medium saucepan, melt butter over medium-high heat. Add bacon, and cook until crisp. Add onion and cook for 2 minutes or until tender. Add clams, clam broth, potatoes, 1 cup potato water, bay leaf, tarragon, thyme, savory, salt, pepper, and cream. Simmer very gently for 5 minutes. Ladle soup into warmed bowls and garnish with a teaspoon of butter. Serves 4.

ENTRÉES

♦ ♦ ♦

H earty and flavorful, serve this colorful omelet for breakfast or lunch with the prerequisite accompaniments: best-quality sausage, bacon, or ham, along with fresh-squeezed orange juice, toast, and homemade jam

POTATO AND SWEET PEPPER OMELET

1 pound (2 large) russet potatoes, peeled and cubed
2 tablespoons olive oil
1 medium-large onion, thinly sliced
2 large garlic cloves, finely chopped
½ cup diced sweet red pepper
¼ cup diced sweet yellow pepper

Salt
Freshly ground black pepper
6 large eggs
1 tablespoon butter
½ cup coarsely chopped fresh flat-leaf parsley
1 cup grated mozzarella or Monterey Jack cheese
2 tablespoons freshly grated Parmesan cheese

BOIL POTATOES in water to cover for 7 minutes or just until tender; drain well.

Heat oil in large nonstick skillet over medium-high heat. Add onion and cook for 2 minutes or until tender. Add garlic, peppers, potatoes, salt and pepper and cook for 3 minutes or until peppers are tender.

Beat eggs lightly with salt and pepper in bowl.

Stir butter into potato mixture and when melted, pour in eggs and tilt pan to spread evenly. Sprinkle parsley over top, reduce heat to medium-low and cook omelet until almost set. Sprinkle with mozzarella and Parmesan cheese and place under preheated broiler for 1 minute or until cheese is melted and bubbly, but not browned (and egg is cooked in center, but not overcooked). Cut in wedges and serve. Serves 6.

SPICY SHEPHERD'S PIE

2 tablespoons butter
1 large onion, chopped
1 sweet red pepper, seeded
  and diced
1½ pounds ground beef
¾ cup canned beef broth
3 tablespoons HP Sauce
Scant 1 tablespoon dried
  thyme
1 teaspoon freshly ground
  black pepper

½ teaspoon dried basil
½ teaspoon ground savory
½ teaspoon salt
¼ teaspoon ground cloves
1 tablespoon cornstarch
  mixed with 1 tablespoon
  water
Whipped Potatoes with
  Wild Mushrooms
  (page 47).

MELT BUTTER in large nonstick skillet over medium-high heat. Add onion and red pepper and cook for 2 minutes or until tender. Add beef and cook, breaking up lumps with a fork, until no pink remains; drain excess fat.

Add beef stock, HP sauce, thyme, pepper, basil, savory, salt, and cloves. Stir to combine, then bring to a simmer. Restir cornstarch mixture, add to meat mixture, and cook until slightly thickened. Spoon into 1½-quart casserole. Spread potato mixture over meat, smoothing with a fork while making a decorative pattern. Bake in 400°F oven for 30 minutes or until filling is hot and topping is golden. Serves 4 to 6.

G round beef cooked with plenty of herbs and spices and topped with a generous amount of mashed or whipped potatoes is appealing wintertime family fare. To dress it up for company, I simply divide the beef mixture into attractive individual-sized ovenproof dishes and pipe the potatoes decoratively on top. ◆ I like to top my pie with Whipped Potatoes with Wild Mushrooms, but for a simpler version, just omit the wild mushrooms. Or try topping the pie with Mashed Potatoes with Blue Cheese (page 49).

I like to serve these feather-light "pasta" dumplings with two sauces – one for blue cheese lovers like myself – the other of tomatoes deliciously punctuated with fresh basil. ◆ The secret to tender gnocchi is to knead in only as much flour as is necessary to produce a workable dough. ◆ Once the gnocchi are cooked they must be served immediately, but the dough can be prepared a day in advance, wrapped tightly in plastic wrap, and refrigerated; or the gnocchi can be formed, covered, and refrigerated for up to 3 hours; or freeze them on foil-lined cookie sheets. Transfer solid gnocchi to freezer bags where they will keep for 1 week. Don't thaw before cooking.

POTATO GNOCCHI WITH TWO SAUCES

3 pounds (6 large) russet potatoes, baked until tender, flesh scooped out and mashed

2 extra-large egg yolks

2 tablespoons butter, melted

About 1½ cups all-purpose flour

1 teaspoon salt

TOMATO BASIL SAUCE

28-ounce can Italian plum tomatoes, undrained

5½-ounce can tomato paste

¼ cup (2 ounces/½ stick) butter

½ cup coarsely chopped fresh basil leaves

¼ teaspoon sugar

Salt

Freshly ground black pepper

GORGONZOLA SAUCE

1½ cups whipping cream

1 cup crumbled Gorgonzola or other blue cheese

3 tablespoons freshly grated Romano or Parmesan cheese

2 tablespoons butter, at room temperature

Freshly grated Romano or Parmesan cheese for serving

SET ASIDE MASHED POTATOES to cool but while still quite warm, stir in egg yolks, butter, 1½ cups flour, and salt until well combined. Transfer to lightly floured surface. Knead dough, adding more flour – 2 tablespoons at a time – only if it's too sticky to handle. Don't overknead dough or it will be heavy.

Divide dough into 8 equal pieces; roll each into 18-inch long cylinder. Cut each cylinder into ¾-inch dumplings. Place a fork tine side down and roll each dumpling down fork to create ribbed indentations (this helps sauce adhere to dumplings).

Prepare sauces while bringing large pot of water to a boil. Tomato Basil Sauce: pureé tomatoes in food processor, push tomatoes through a strainer into nonreactive saucepan to remove seeds. Stir in tomato paste, butter, ½ the basil, sugar, salt, and pepper and simmer 20 minutes; stir in remaining basil. Gorgonzola Sauce: bring cream to a boil in medium saucepan, reduce heat, and simmer a few minutes or until slightly thickened. Add cheeses and stir until smooth.

Add about tablespoon salt to boiling water, carefully add gnocchi, stirring with wooden spoon to prevent sticking, and cook for 3 minutes or until they all rise to surface.

Add 2 tablespoons butter to warmed serving bowl. Transfer gnocchi to serving bowl with slotted spoon and toss with butter. Serve accompanied by the two sauces. Pass extra grated cheese and the peppermill. Serves 6 to 8.

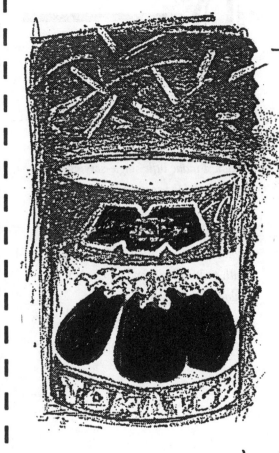

canned
tomatoes

SALMON AND POTATO PIE

Red salmon combined with mashed potatoes, fresh rosemary, and parsley and baked in a crust is an excellent winter supper dish. For a fancier presentation, I make little single-serving-size tartlets. ♦ Do use canned red – not pink – salmon for best flavor and color. If you can't get fresh rosemary, just omit it – don't substitute dried. ♦ Serve the pie with pickled beets and a tossed green salad or tiny green peas.

1 can (7.5-ounces) red salmon, drained, reserving liquid
¼ cup (2 ounces/½ stick) butter
1¾ cups chopped onions
¼ cup all-purpose flour
About ¾ cup milk
2 pounds (4 large) russet potatoes, peeled and cubed
1 large garlic clove, peeled
¾ cup milk
½ cup chopped fresh parsley
2 teaspoons coarsely chopped fresh rosemary
½ teaspoon salt
½ teaspoon freshly ground black pepper
Pastry for 1-crust pie (page 42)
1 tablespoon milk, for glaze

REMOVE AND DISCARD skin and large bones from drained salmon; set aside.

Melt butter in heavy medium saucepan over medium-high heat. Add onions and cook for 2 minutes or until tender. Stir in flour and cook, stirring constantly, for 2 minutes.

Measure reserved salmon liquid and add enough milk to make 1 cup liquid; add to onion mixture, whisking constantly for several seconds or until thickened; remove from heat.

Meanwhile, boil potatoes and garlic in water to cover until tender; drain. Mash potatoes and garlic with ¾ cup milk until smooth and lump-free and stir in onion mixture until well combined. Gently stir in salmon chunks, parsley, rosemary, salt, and pepper. Spoon salmon mixture into a 9-inch glass pie plate. Roll out pastry to form a 10-inch circle and place over salmon mixture. Trim pastry even with rim of pan. Crimp and seal edges. Cut steam vents and cut out fish-shapes from dough trimmings to decorate top of crust. Chill for at least 30 minutes. Just before baking brush pie crust lightly with milk. Bake in a preheated 400°F oven for 45 minutes or until top is golden and filling hot. Serves 6.

SEAFOOD POTATO PIE

1 tablespoon butter, at room temperature
1 tablespoon all-purpose flour
1½ cups water
1 pound (2 large) russet potatoes, peeled and diced
2 medium carrots, diced
1 small celery stalk, finely diced
1 medium onion, chopped
½ pound sea scallops, cut into large dice
½ pound large shrimp, peeled, deveined, and cut into large dice
1½ teaspoons dried tarragon
1 teaspoon dried thyme
Salt
Freshly ground black pepper
½ cup half-and-half
Pastry for 2-crust pie (page 42)

MAKE A BEURRE MANIÉ: stir butter and flour in small bowl until thoroughly combined; set aside.

Bring water to a boil in large saucepan over medium-high heat. Add potatoes, carrots, celery, and onion. Reduce heat to medium-low and simmer for 5 minutes or until vegetables are just tender. Add scallops, shrimp, tarragon, thyme, salt, and pepper and cook for 2 minutes or until opaque; do not overcook. Stir in half-and-half, then beurre manié, and cook for 1 minute or until just thickened; remove from heat.

Roll out half the pastry to fit bottom of 11-inch pie plate and line bottom and sides with pastry. Pour filling into pastry-lined dish.

Roll out remaining pastry and cut into 1-inch strips, using a jagged-edged pastry wheel. Arrange strips in a lattice design on top of mixture. Bake in preheated 400°F oven for 30 minutes or until pastry is golden and filling is hot. Serves 4 to 6.

*L*uxurious seafood with cream, bites of potato, carrot, and celery, sprinkled with tarragon and thyme, and baked in a flaky pie crust, is nothing short of blissful.
♦ *The perfect complement: homemade tomato relish and a tossed green salad.*

Chickpeas and potatoes cooked in a basil-scented tomato sauce is a rustic combo that's easy to make and unexpectedly delicious. ◆ With some crusty bread and a crisp green salad, this makes a good, hearty meal.

CHICKPEA AND POTATO STEW

¼ cup olive oil
1 medium onion, chopped
2 large garlic cloves, chopped
¼ teaspoon hot red pepper flakes
28-ounce can Italian plum tomatoes, undrained
1 pound (2 large) russet potatoes, cut into ½-inch cubes (no larger)

19-ounce can chickpeas, drained
1 cup fresh basil leaves, coarsely chopped
1 teaspoon dried basil
Salt
Freshly ground black pepper
Freshly grated Parmesan cheese for serving

HEAT OIL in large nonstick or nonreactive skillet over medium-high heat. Add onion, garlic, and pepper flakes and cook for 2 minutes or until tender. Add tomatoes, including liquid, potatoes, chickpeas, ¼ cup fresh basil, dried basil, salt, and pepper and bring to a boil. Reduce heat to medium-low, cover, and simmer for 20 minutes or until potatoes are tender and sauce is thickened. Just before serving, stir in the remaining basil. Serve in wide shallow bowls with Parmesan cheese. Serves 6.

GREEK CHICKEN AND POTATOES

¼ cup olive oil
6 skinless chicken thighs
8 large garlic cloves, peeled and left whole
1¼ cups chicken stock
1 medium lemon, unpeeled, thinly sliced, and seeds removed

About 3 large russet potatoes, peeled, quartered lengthwise, then cut in half crosswise
2 teaspoons dried oregano
Salt
Freshly ground black pepper

HEAT OIL in large nonstick or nonreactive skillet over medium-high heat. Add chicken and garlic and cook for 2 minutes or until chicken is lightly browned. Add chicken stock, lemon slices, and as many potato chunks as will fit in skillet and be completely covered with stock. Sprinkle with oregano, salt, and pepper and bring to a boil. Reduce heat to medium-low, cover, and simmer for 1 hour, stirring frequently, or until potatoes are tender and chicken is cooked through. Serves 3 to 4.

Greek chicken and potato stew is a tangy, easy-to-prepare dish. A simple green salad – or a Greek salad with feta cheese and Kalamata olives – and crusty bread would complete the meal.

Mexican pork and chile stew typically includes "posole" – corn that has been removed from the cob and specially treated, then dried. I've replaced the posole with potatoes for a similar flavor effect. ◆ To make the stew really special, serve bowls of coarsely chopped ripe cherry tomatoes, diced avocado tossed with a little lime juice, chopped fresh coriander, and chopped green onion to add at the table.

PORK, CHILE, AND POTATO STEW

3 pounds boneless pork shoulder or butt, trimmed and cut into 1-inch cubes
4 large garlic cloves, chopped
1 medium-large onion, chopped
2½ cups chicken stock
2 cups water
2 teaspoons dried oregano
1 teaspoon salt
1 pound (2 large) russet potatoes, peeled and cut into 1-inch cubes

1 medium-large zucchini, trimmed, unpeeled, halved lengthwise, and cut into ½-inch thick slices
10-ounce package frozen whole kernel corn
2 tablespoons chopped pickled sliced jalapeños
½ cup chopped fresh coriander
Quartered limes for garnish

BRING PORK, garlic, onion, chicken stock, and water to a boil in large saucepan. Reduce heat to medium-low, cover, and simmer for 1 hour or until pork is tender. Skim off most – but not all – of surface fat from stock.

Add oregano, salt, and potatoes; cover and cook for 20 minutes or just until tender. Add zucchini, corn, and chiles; cook another 20 minutes or until tender. Stir in coriander and serve with lime wedges. Serves 6.

BREAKFAST SAUSAGE
WITH POTATO AND RED PEPPER

1 tablespoon olive oil
1 pound best-quality pork
  sausage, cut into 1-inch
  thick slices
1 pound (2 large) russet
  potatoes, peeled and
  cubed
1 large sweet red pepper,
  seeded and cut into
  1-inch pieces

1 fennel bulb, trimmed and
  cut into 1-inch pieces
1 medium red onion, cut
  into 1-inch pieces
Salt
Freshly ground black
  pepper

HEAT OIL in large nonstick skillet over medium-high heat. Add sausage and cook for 5 minutes or until beginning to brown. Remove and discard as much oil as possible. Add potatoes, red pepper, fennel, red onion, salt, and pepper. Cover, reduce heat to medium-low, and cook, stirring frequently and spooning out any excess oil, for 45 minutes or until potatoes are tender and sausage is cooked through. Remove cover, turn heat to medium-high, and cook for a few more minutes until potatoes are golden and lightly crisped. Serves 6.

*I*n this homey dish, breakfast sausage is sautéed with potatoes, red peppers, fennel, and red onion for a hearty accompaniment to eggs. ◆ Purchase freshly-made sausage from a farmers' market or quality butcher for best flavor.

L ard is my preference for pie pastry – I really appreciate its old-fashioned flavor. ♦ This is a wonderful crust for both sweet or savory pies.

FLAKY PASTRY

2½ cups all-purpose flour
1 teaspoon salt
1 cup (8 ounces) lard
About ½ cup ice water

COMBINE FLOUR and salt in food processor. Add lard in big chunks, stirring to coat each chunk with flour before processing. Process mixture for only a few seconds – until lard becomes the size of large lima beans. Working very quickly, turn on machine and add ice water through feed tube and process only until combined. Remove to lightly floured surface and knead just until dough forms into a smooth ball. Divide dough in two, then slightly flatten each ball into a round disk. Completely enclose each disk in plastic wrap, chill, and use as directed in recipe. Makes enough for 1 double-crust 9-inch pie or 2 single-crust pies.

MASHED, BAKED & STEAMED

♦ ♦ ♦

D*ouble-baked stuffed potatoes can be served as a light lunch or snack, or enjoyed as a hearty side dish to a light meal.*

CHEESE-STUFFED BAKED POTATOES

1 pound (2 large) russet
   potatoes, scrubbed
⅓ cup sour cream
1 tablespoon milk
½ cup grated sharp white
   Cheddar cheese, plus
   2 tablespoons

2 tablespoons chopped
   chives or green onion
   (green part only)
Salt
Freshly ground black
   pepper

PREHEAT OVEN to 425°F.

Bake potatoes for 1 hour or until tender. When cool enough to handle but still warm, slice a ½-inch thick piece lengthwise off top of each potato; scoop out flesh, leaving ¼-inch shell.

Mash potato flesh with sour cream, milk, cheese, chives, salt, and pepper. Spoon mixture back into potato skins; place them on baking sheet and bake for 8 minutes or until heated through. Serves 2.

ROASTED POTATOES WITH GARLIC AND ROSEMARY

1½ pounds medium white potatoes, unpeeled, cut into eighths
10 to 15 large garlic cloves, peeled and left whole
¼ cup olive oil
1 generous tablespoon fresh rosemary leaves
Salt
Freshly ground black pepper

PREHEAT OVEN to 400°F.
  Combine potatoes, garlic, olive oil, rosemary, salt, and pepper in a 1½-quart baking dish. Bake for 1 hour or until potatoes are tender and golden, stirring occasionally. Serves 4 to 6.

Garlic devotees will find this dish terrific. The potatoes become flavored with the fragrant bulb, while the garlic itself becomes deliciously sweet and caramelized. A wonderful side dish to roasted or grilled poultry, meat, fish, or seafood.

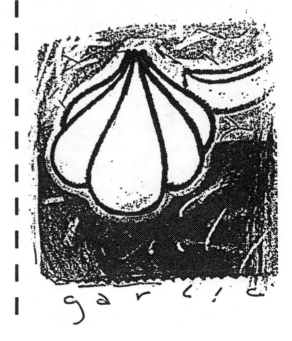

garlic

*S*erve these potatoes when you're in a hurry and want baked potatoes in a little less time. Besides, they have a more refined appearance than a whole baked potato.

HALVED BAKED POTATOES

2 large baking potatoes,
   well scrubbed and cut in
   half lengthwise

PREHEAT OVEN to 400°F.
   Place potatoes cut side up on baking sheet or right on oven rack. Bake for 40 minutes or until tender and tops have puffed up and formed a golden brown crust. (Be careful not to overcook or potato will dry out.) Serves 2 to 4.

WHIPPED POTATOES
WITH WILD MUSHROOMS

2½ pounds (5 large) russet
   potatoes, peeled and
   cubed
½ cup (4 ounces/1 stick)
   butter
6 ounces fresh shiitake
   mushrooms, stemmed,
   quickly rinsed, dried,
   and coarsely chopped

½ cup warm milk
1 teaspoon salt
Lots of freshly ground black
   pepper

BOIL POTATOES in water to cover for 8 minutes or until tender.

Meanwhile, melt butter in medium skillet over medium heat. Add mushrooms and cook for 2 minutes or until tender; do not overcook. Keep warm.

Drain potatoes well and place in heavy-duty mixer (not a food processor or they'll turn gummy). Using whisk attachment, on low speed, beat potatoes until mashed. Add mushroom mixture, milk, salt, and pepper and continue beating, turning up speed gradually until on medium speed. Continue beating for 1 minute or until fluffy.

Alternately, mash potatoes with potato masher until smooth and lump free, or pass through a ricer and stir in remaining ingredients. Makes about 6 cups.

omey mashed potatoes are combined with wild mushrooms for a wonderful balance of earthiness and sophistication. ◆ Excellent as a side dish to beef, poultry, or game, they also make a perfect topping for Spicy Shepherds Pie (page 33).

While lighter than mashed potatoes made just with butter, remember these will only be as good as your olive oil. ◆ Use the best oil – taste it first to make sure the flavor of the oil is exactly what you want to impart to the potatoes.

MASHED POTATOES WITH GARLIC AND OLIVE OIL

2 pounds (4 large) russet or Yukon Gold potatoes, peeled and quartered
4 large garlic cloves, unpeeled
½ cup warm milk
1 teaspoon salt
Lots of freshly ground black pepper
¼ cup best-quality olive oil
2 tablespoons butter, at room temperature

BOIL POTATOES and garlic in water to cover for 15 minutes or until tender; drain well and peel garlic.

Pass garlic and potatoes through a ricer, or mash with potato masher, or whip in heavy-duty mixer (not a food processor) until smooth. Add milk, salt, pepper, and olive oil and continue mashing until fluffy. Transfer to serving bowl, make a well in the top of mixture and add butter; stir it in at the table. Serves 4.

MASHED POTATOES
WITH BLUE CHEESE

2 pounds (4 large) russet
  potatoes, peeled and
  cubed
½ cup warm milk
¼ cup (2 ounces / ½ stick)
  butter, at room
  temperature
1 green onion (green part
  only) finely chopped

Salt
Freshly ground black
  pepper
½ cup blue cheese,
  crumbled
Freshly grated nutmeg

BOIL POTATOES in water to cover for 8 minutes or until tender; drain well. Whip or mash potatoes until smooth with heavy-duty mixer (not a food processor) or potato masher, or pass through a ricer.

Add milk and butter and mash until fluffy. Stir in green onion, salt, pepper, and blue cheese. Spoon onto warmed plates and grate a little nutmeg on top. Serves 4.

Tangy blue cheese is a wonderful addition to hot, creamy, fluffy mashed potatoes. ◆ *Great as a topping for Shepherd's Pie, too.*

Potato-Onion Dressing is a very old French-Canadian recipe with generous amounts of savory, sage, and pepper. It's a robust-flavored dressing tradition-ally served (with plenty of gravy!) with the Christmas turkey. ◆ Feel free to decrease the herbs and spices and to not wait until Christmas to try it! ◆ The giblets are ground through a meat grinder – not in a food processor – for the right texture.

POTATO-ONION TURKEY DRESSING

3 tablespoons butter
2 large garlic cloves, chopped
2 large onions, finely chopped
Turkey giblets, ground
5 cups unseasoned mashed potatoes (5 large russets)
1 teaspoon crumbled dried sage

½ teaspoon ground savory
1 teaspoon salt
1 teaspoon freshly ground black pepper
¼ cup (2 ounces/½ stick) melted butter
1 large egg, lightly beaten

MELT 3 TABLESPOONS butter in large nonstick skillet. Add garlic and onions and cook for 3 minutes or until tender. Add giblets and cook for 3 minutes or until cooked through.

Combine giblet mixture with mashed potatoes, sage, savory, salt, pepper, melted butter, and egg in large bowl until thoroughly blended. Spoon into casserole, cover, and bake alongside the turkey for 40 minutes or until heated through. Serves 8 to 10 when served with all the turkey trimmings.

TANGY MASHED POTATOES

2 pounds (4 large) russet
  potatoes, peeled and
  cubed
About ½ cup yogurt or
  buttermilk, at room
  temperature
¼ cup (2 ounces/½ stick)
  butter, at room
  temperature

1 teaspoon salt
Lots of freshly ground black
  pepper
¼ cup chopped chives
  or green onion (green
  part only)

BOIL POTATOES in water to cover for 8 minutes or until tender; drain well. Whip potatoes until smooth with heavy-duty mixer (not a food processor) or mash with potato masher, or pass through a ricer.

Add yogurt or buttermilk, butter, salt, and pepper and continue to mash until fluffy. Transfer to serving bowl and sprinkle with chives. Serves 4.

Y*ogurt, or buttermilk, adds a delicate tang to mashed potatoes.* ♦ *If you would like more richness and creaminess (and more calories!), simply substitute sour cream.*

Piquant Potato Cakes get their distinctive taste from sun-dried tomatoes, Kalamata olives, and capers. ♦ Make them with leftover potato flesh from making potato skins or boil and mash two large russets. ♦ Go easy on the salt: capers, sun-dried tomatoes, and olives are often salty.

Piquant Potato Cakes

2 cups unseasoned mashed potatoes
2 large whole sun-dried tomatoes in olive oil, drained and diced
2 tablespoons drained tiny capers
6 Greek olives (Kalamata), pitted and coarsely chopped

1 large egg, lightly beaten
Salt
Freshly ground black pepper
About 2 tablespoons heavy cream (optional)
About 3 tablespoons all-purpose flour
Olive oil or butter for frying

Combine potatoes, sun-dried tomatoes, capers, olives, egg, salt, and pepper in medium bowl. Take a little of the potato mixture, form into a small patty, then lightly dust with flour and fry in a little oil to check seasoning. If you would like more moisture in the potato cakes, add some heavy cream to the mixture.

Form the remaining mixture into 1-inch balls, then flatten into patties and lightly dust with flour.

Heat about 1 tablespoon oil or butter in large nonstick skillet over medium-high heat. Cook patties, in batches if necessary, adding more oil as needed, for 3 minutes or until golden colored on both sides and heated through. Makes about 16 potato cakes.

CHEESY MASHED POTATOES

4 cups warm unseasoned
   mashed potatoes
   (4 large russets)
¾ cup sour cream
4 ounces cream cheese,
   at room temperature
¼ cup (2 ounces/½ stick)
   butter, at room
   temperature

1 teaspoon salt
Freshly ground black
   pepper
1 cup shredded Cheddar
   cheese (4 ounces)

THOROUGHLY COMBINE potatoes, sour cream, cream cheese, butter, salt, and pepper in large bowl, using a potato masher or heavy-duty mixer (not a food processor). Spoon mixture into baking dish, sprinkle with Cheddar cheese. Cover and bake in preheated 400°F oven for 20 minutes. Remove cover and bake for 8 minutes more. Serves 4 to 6.

Velvety mashed potatoes baked with Cheddar and cream cheese is especially delicious. ◆ Wonderful with meatloaf, fried chicken, pepper steak and the like – or simply all on its own!

L ight on cholesterol and fat, this virtuous variation on cream-laden gratins combines potatoes with chicken stock and grated Parmesan cheese.

POTATO GRATIN WITH PARMESAN CHEESE

2 pounds (4 large) russet potatoes, peeled and thinly sliced
Salt
Freshly ground black pepper

1 large garlic clove, finely chopped
6 tablespoons freshly grated Parmesan cheese
1½ cups chicken stock

PREHEAT OVEN to 400°F.

Lightly grease oval gratin dish and arrange a layer of potatoes on bottom. Sprinkle with salt, pepper, ⅓ garlic, and 2 tablespoons cheese. Repeat twice more and pour over stock.

Bake for 45 minutes to 1 hour, stirring potato mixture every 20 minutes or so, or until potatoes are tender.

Place under broiler for 4 minutes or until top becomes golden brown. Serves 4.

POTATO GRATIN
WITH THYME AND TARRAGON

2 pounds (4 large) russet
   potatoes, peeled and
   thinly sliced
2 tablespoons butter, diced
2 large garlic cloves,
   coarsely chopped
1 teaspoon dried tarragon

¼ teaspoon dried thyme
½ teaspoon salt
½ teaspoon freshly ground
   black pepper
½ teaspoon grated nutmeg
1½ cups heavy cream

PREHEAT OVEN to 400°F.

Place potato slices in lightly greased oval gratin dish. Scatter butter and garlic cloves over potatoes. Sprinkle with tarragon, thyme, salt, pepper, and nutmeg. Pour over cream and stir to distribute seasonings evenly.

Bake for 45 minutes to 1 hour or until cream is absorbed into potatoes and edges are buttery, stirring potatoes every 20 minutes or so – each time the top becomes lightly browned and has formed a crust. Continually stirring the browned crust into the potatoes gives them exceptional flavor. Serves 6.

H*eavy cream is essential to this extraordinarily rich and delicious dish.* ♦ *I don't recommend substituting light cream or milk to cut calories, just have smaller helpings!* ♦ *The gratin is best fresh from the oven, but you can combine all of the ingredients in a baking dish, cover, and refrigerate a few hours before baking.*

Anchovy lovers will delight in this creamy, richly flavored potato concoction of Scandinavian origin, aptly named Jansson's Temptation.

POTATO GRATIN
WITH ANCHOVIES AND ONION

1½ pounds (3 large) russet or Yukon Gold potatoes, peeled and thinly sliced
Salt
Freshly ground black pepper
1 large onion, thinly sliced

2-ounce (50g) can anchovies, drained, patted dry, and coarsely chopped
1¼ cups heavy cream
3 tablespoons dry bread crumbs

PREHEAT OVEN to 400°F.

Lightly grease oval gratin dish and arrange half of potatoes on the bottom. Sprinkle lightly with salt and pepper, then layer onions and anchovies over potatoes. Top with remaining potatoes, sprinkle with salt and pepper, and pour over heavy cream. Sprinkle with bread crumbs, and bake for 40 minutes or until potatoes are tender and casserole is bubbly and brown on top. Serves 4.

POTATO GRATIN WITH BLUE CHEESE

2 pounds (4 large) russet
  potatoes, peeled and
  thinly sliced
½ pound Gorgonzola,
  Cambozola, or other
  mild blue cheese (rind
  removed)

Salt
Freshly ground black
  pepper
3 tablespoons freshly
  grated Parmesan cheese
1½ cups heavy cream
Large pinch grated nutmeg

PREHEAT OVEN to 400°F.

Lightly grease oval gratin dish and arrange a layer of potatoes on bottom. Dot potatoes with ⅓ blue cheese, sprinkle with a little salt, pepper, and 1 tablespoon Parmesan cheese. Repeat twice more, pour over cream, and sprinkle top with nutmeg. Bake for 45 minutes to 1 hour or until almost all the cream is absorbed and potatoes are tender. Serves 4 to 6.

An absolutely foolproof gratin with character, this time the potatoes are baked in a creamy Gorgonzola mixture. It's positively charismatic for blue cheese devotees – like me!

cheese grater

5 7

C risp on the outside and buttery-flavored, these potatoes make a delicious accompaniment to roast chicken, beef, or lamb.

OVEN-FRIED POTATO SLICES

¼ cup (2 ounces/½ stick) butter
2 large russet potatoes, peeled and cut into ¼-inch slices

Salt
Freshly ground black pepper

PREHEAT OVEN to 450°F.

Place butter in 10- x 15-inch jelly roll pan and put in oven for a minute or until butter is melted. Remove from oven and arrange potato slices in one layer in pan. Sprinkle lightly with salt and pepper. Bake for 15 minutes or until crisp and golden on one side. Turn over with flat spatula and cook another 10 minutes or until tender and crisp. Transfer to serving dish – leaving any excess butter behind – and serve at once. Serves 2 to 4.

SNOWBALLS

1½ pounds (3 large) russet potatoes, peeled and cubed
3 tablespoons butter
1 medium onion, chopped
½ teaspoon salt
¼ teaspoon freshly ground black pepper

½ cup fine dry bread crumbs
½ teaspoon crumbled, dried sage (if serving with poultry)
1 large egg yolk, lightly beaten

BOIL POTATOES in water to cover for 8 minutes or just until tender; drain well. Place in bowl and mash until smooth and lump free; set aside.

Melt butter in heavy medium skillet over medium-high heat. Add onion and cook for 1 minute or until tender. Stir onion into potatoes. Add salt, pepper, and bread crumbs (and sage if using) and thoroughly combine. If mixture seems dry, add another tablespoon or so of melted butter.

When cool enough to handle but while still warm, form mixture into 1½-inch balls; place on well-buttered baking sheet. Brush tops and sides of potato balls with beaten egg yolk. Bake in preheated 425°F oven for 25 minutes or until golden. Makes about 26 potato balls.

*D*elightfully old-fashioned, snowballs are simply bright-yellow potato balls. The potato mixture is formed into small balls which are painted with egg yolk before baking. ◆ This recipe is from my mother's friend, Alice Ainsworth, and came, in turn, from her French-Canadian mother. Alice's mother always flavored the mixture with a little sage when serving them with poultry.

A *simple formulation to make the tasty little taters even more tempting!*

HERBED NEW POTATOES

¾ pound small new potatoes

2 tablespoons butter, at room temperature

1 generous tablespoon minced fresh parsley

1 generous tablespoon minced fresh basil

1 tablespoon snipped fresh chives

1 teaspoon finely grated lemon zest

Salt

Freshly ground black pepper

STEAM POTATOES on a steaming rack over boiling water, covered, for 10 to 15 minutes (depending on size of potatoes) or until tender. Toss potatoes with butter and herbs, lemon zest, salt, and pepper in bowl until coated evenly. Serves 2 to 4.

From Italy comes this uncomplicated accompaniment for all things grilled.

BAKED POTATOES AND TOMATOES

1½ pounds (6 medium) white potatoes, thinly sliced
1 large onion, thinly sliced
2 large garlic cloves, chopped
1 pound ripe plum tomatoes, thinly sliced

¼ cup olive oil
1 teaspoon dried basil
Salt
Freshly ground black pepper

PREHEAT OVEN to 400°F.

Combine potatoes, onion, garlic, tomatoes, oil, basil, salt, and pepper in 9- x 13-inch baking dish. Cover with foil and bake for 55 minutes, stirring occasionally, until potatoes are tender. Serves 6.

potatoes

POTATO SALADS

♦ ♦ ♦

J

ust because I happen to prefer the mealy-textured baking potato in my potato salads, doesn't mean you can't substitute your favorite waxy spuds – either white or unpeeled red. ◆ Fresh basil and full-of-flavor tomatoes are essential to this light dish.

POTATO SALAD WITH FRESH BASIL AND TOMATOES

2 pounds (4 large) russet potatoes, peeled and cubed
1 garlic clove, finely chopped
¼ cup chopped white onion
¼ cup light olive oil
2 tablespoons red wine vinegar
½ teaspoon dried basil
Salt
Freshly ground black pepper
2 medium-large (1 pound) fresh, ripe tomatoes, seeded and diced
½ cup coarsely chopped fresh basil leaves

BOIL POTATOES in water to cover for 8 minutes or just until tender; drain well. Place in large bowl, and while warm, stir in garlic, onion, oil, vinegar, dried basil, salt, and pepper. Allow to cool until lukewarm, then stir in tomatoes and fresh basil. Serve at room temperature or lightly chilled. Serves 4 to 6.

POTATO SALAD WITH BLUE CHEESE AND PECANS

2 pounds (4 large) russet potatoes peeled, or unpeeled red potatoes, cubed
2 tablespoons dry white vermouth
2 tablespoons cider vinegar
½ cup mayonnaise
2 generous tablespoons sour cream
1 tablespoon Dijon mustard
½ cup pecan halves, lightly toasted and coarsely chopped
1 large whole green onion, chopped
1 cup crumbled blue cheese
Salt
Freshly ground black pepper

BOIL POTATOES in water to cover for 8 minutes or just until tender; drain well and place in large bowl. While hot, toss potatoes with vermouth and cider vinegar; allow to cool to room temperature.

Add mayonnaise, sour cream, mustard, pecans, green onion, blue cheese, salt, and pepper and stir until combined. Serve at room temperature or lightly chilled. Serves 4 to 6.

Yes, I love blue cheese and if you do, too, you'll simply adore this captivating creation. ◆ Use either red potatoes – they look more attractive in their red skins, or my favorite – russets.

You won't miss the mayonnaise or the calories! Casting custom aside, here potatoes are combined with two mustards – Dijon and whole grain – for an updated, low-cholesterol taste treat.

mustard

RED POTATO SALAD WITH TWO MUSTARDS

2 pounds red potatoes, unpeeled and cut into cubes
1/3 cup red or white onion, chopped
2 tablespoons Dijon mustard

2 to 3 tablespoons whole-grain mustard
1/4 cup olive oil
1/2 teaspoon salt
Freshly ground black pepper

BOIL POTATOES in water to cover for 8 minutes or until tender; drain well. Place in large bowl, and while hot, stir in onion, mustards, olive oil, salt, and pepper until well combined. Chill for several hours, then bring back to room temperature before serving. Serves 4 to 6.

POTATO SALAD WITH SMOKED SALMON, CAPERS, AND GREEN BEANS

1½ pounds (3 large) russet potatoes, peeled and cubed
½ pound green beans, trimmed and cut into 1-inch pieces
1 tablespoon olive oil
1 tablespoon tarragon vinegar
2 tablespoons chopped fresh tarragon
2 tablespoons drained tiny capers
1 teaspoon salt
1 cup mayonnaise
3 ounces best-quality, thinly-sliced smoked salmon, cut into ½-inch strips

BOIL POTATOES in water to cover for 8 minutes or just until tender; transfer to large bowl with slotted spoon reserving boiling water. Add green beans to boiling water and cook for 4 minutes or until tender but still bright green; plunge beans into ice water to chill, then drain and pat dry with paper towels.

While hot, toss potatoes with oil and vinegar. Allow to cool, then add green beans, tarragon, capers, salt, and mayonnaise and stir to combine. Gently stir in smoked salmon. Chill until ready to serve. Serves 4 to 6.

Spectacular! A lavish, elegant salad of pale smoked salmon contrasting with creamy mayonnaise, fluffy-textured potatoes, tender green beans, and tangy capers. ◆ This bounteous blend is nothing but blissful.

W onderful flavors, textures, and colors – soft, crumbly cubes of russet potatoes, chunks of vivid red pimentos, bites of crisp, sweet gherkins, and bright yellow flecks of yolk – all tossed together in a tangy mayonnaise – create a sensational potato salad, indeed! ◆ Pimentos are available in supermarkets, usually in the pickle section next to the capers and the like.

PERFECT POTATO SALAD

1½ pounds (3 large) russet or Yukon Gold potatoes, peeled and cubed
3 tablespoons sweet gherkin pickle juice
8 sweet gherkins, coarsely chopped
¼ cup finely chopped white onion
2 hard-boiled eggs, very finely chopped

2 jars (each 4.5 ounces) pimentos, drained well and roughly cut into 1 to 2-inch pieces
1 teaspoon salt
Freshly ground black pepper
1 cup mayonnaise

BOIL POTATOES in water to cover for 8 minutes or just until tender; drain well. Place in large bowl, and while hot, stir in pickle juice until absorbed. Allow to cool, then add gherkins, onion, eggs, pimentos, salt, pepper, and mayonnaise and gently stir until well combined. Cover and chill until ready to serve. Serves 4 to 6.

GREEK-STYLE POTATO SALAD

1½ pounds (3 large) russet potatoes, peeled and cubed
1 tablespoon olive oil
1 tablespoon red wine vinegar
1 garlic clove, finely chopped
1 teaspoon dried oregano
¼ cup olive oil
2 tablespoons red wine vinegar
Salt
Freshly ground black pepper
¼ teaspoon dried mint
¼ cup chopped red onion
1 cup Greek olives (Kalamata), pitted and cut into thick slivers
1 ripe medium tomato, seeded and coarsely chopped
1 cup crumbled Feta cheese (about 4 ounces)
½ cup coarsely chopped fresh parsley

BOIL POTATOES in water to cover for 8 minutes or just until tender; drain well. Place in large bowl, and while hot, stir in 1 tablespoon oil, 1 tablespoon vinegar, garlic, and oregano. Allow to cool a little.

Whisk remaining oil, vinegar, salt, pepper, and mint in bowl until emulsified; stir into potato mixture. Add red onion, olives, tomato, cheese, and parsley and stir to combine. Cover, and chill overnight to allow flavors to meld. Serves 4 to 6.

P *ungent Kalamata olives — not canned domestic ones — are a must for this sprightly take on the traditional Greek salad of feta cheese, tomatoes, and olives.* ◆ *The salad should be made a day ahead for the flavors to mellow, so plan accordingly.*

*S*un-dried tomatoes, capers, and fresh mint delightfully enhance this cheerful potato salad. ◆ Use only the brightest red sun-dried tomatoes you can find: they have the most intense tomato flavor – dull-brownish-red ones just won't do. ◆ The most attractive way to serve this salad is to mix in only half the tomatoes and mint and to sprinkle the remainder over the top, turning it all together at the table.

WARM POTATO SALAD WITH SUN-DRIED TOMATOES AND MINT

2 pounds (4 large) russet potatoes, peeled and cubed
¼ cup chopped white onion
¼ cup light olive oil
¼ cup red wine vinegar
½ teaspoon salt
1 large garlic clove, finely chopped

1 tablespoon drained tiny capers
8 large whole sun-dried tomatoes in oil, drained and diced
2 tablespoons roughly chopped fresh mint leaves (not dried)

BOIL POTATOES in water to cover for 8 minutes or just until tender; drain well. Place in large bowl, and while hot, stir in onion, oil, vinegar, salt, garlic, capers, sun-dried tomatoes, and mint until well combined. Serve warm or at room temperature. Serves 4.

SWEET POTATO AND HAM SALAD

1½ pounds (2 medium-large) sweet potatoes, peeled and cubed
¼ cup olive oil
2 tablespoons Dijon mustard
1 tablespoon red wine vinegar

1 teaspoon sugar
½ pound smoked ham, thinly sliced and cut into 1-inch pieces
4-ounce jar pimento pieces, drained well
1 large whole green onion, chopped

BOIL POTATOES in water to cover for 8 minutes or just until tender; drain well. Place in large bowl, and while warm, stir in oil, mustard, vinegar, and sugar. Add ham, pimentos, and green onions and stir until combined. Serve warm or at room temperature. Serves 6.

M ost sweet potato salads are kind of cloying with their usual medley of raisins, fruit, and the like. This salad has only one sweet ingredient – the potatoes themselves. The others – smoked ham, mustard, green onions, and pimentos – add savory notes to this colorful, unusual combination.

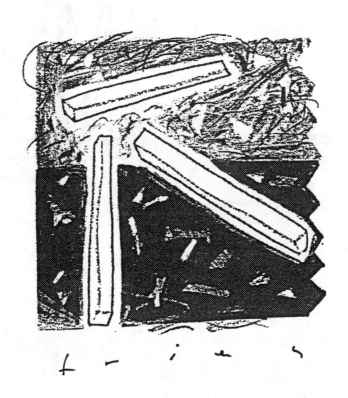

FRIES, OVEN FRIES & SAUTÉED

♦ ♦ ♦

P otatoes and leeks, first sautéed, then "baked" on top of the stove in a covered skillet are wonderful – I love the way the bits of browned leeks complement the potatoes.

POTATOES AND LEEKS

¼ cup (2 ounces/½ stick) butter
2½ cups finely chopped white part of leeks; previously well rinsed
1½ pounds (3 large) russet potatoes, peeled and cut into ½-inch thick slices

¼ teaspoon ground savory
¼ cup water
½ cup finely chopped fresh parsley
¼ teaspoon salt
¼ teaspoon freshly ground black pepper

MELT BUTTER in large nonstick skillet over medium-high heat. Add leeks and cook, stirring, for 4 minutes or until tender. Add potatoes and savory, stirring to thoroughly combine.

Pour in water, cover, and reduce heat to medium-low. Cook, stirring occasionally, for 20 minutes or until potatoes are very tender. (Add a little water – about 1 to 2 table-spoons – if liquid evaporates before potatoes are tender, but don't add too much or they won't brown properly.) When potatoes are tender and lightly browned, stir in parsley, salt, and pepper. Cover and cook another few minutes or until parsley has softened. Serves 4.

LEMONY POTATOES

¼ cup olive oil
1 medium-large onion,
  chopped
2 large garlic cloves,
  chopped
1 tablespoon ground cumin
1 teaspoon mustard seeds
¼ teaspoon hot red pepper
  flakes
2 pounds (4 large) russet or
  Yukon Gold potatoes,
  peeled and cut into
  ½-inch thick slices

Finely grated zest of
  1 medium lemon
¼ cup fresh lemon juice
1 cup water
¼ teaspoon salt
2 tablespoons finely
  chopped fresh coriander
  (optional)

HEAT OIL in large nonstick or nonreactive skillet over medium-high heat. Stir in onion, garlic, cumin, mustard seeds, and red pepper flakes and cook for 1 minute or until fragrant. Add potatoes and stir to coat with seasonings. Add lemon zest, lemon juice, water, and salt and bring to a boil. Reduce heat to medium-low, cover, and cook, turning occasionally, for 30 minutes or until potatoes are very tender and liquid is absorbed. Sprinkle with coriander and serve. Serves 4.

J oyously tangy with lemon, garlic, cumin, and onion, this Moroccan dish "baked" in a skillet is delicious served as a side dish, or enjoy in the traditional Moroccan manner – accompanied by a dollop of plain yogurt and a green salad – as a vegetarian meal.

A breakfast of bacon, eggs, toast, jam – the works – is an occasional treat at our house. But when we do indulge, we feel a to-heck-with-cholesterol breakfast just doesn't cut it without home fries. Maybe it's because of all those years of journeying by car, devouring breakfast after gratifying breakfast in countless diners! ♦ To my taste, pale golden, somewhat soft-textured home fries cooked in butter are best. My better half prefers his fried in vegetable oil for a much crisper result. Either way is delicious.

HEAVENLY HOME FRIES

2 pounds (4 large) russet or
  Yukon Gold potatoes,
  peeled and cut into
  ¾-inch cubes
About ¼ cup (2 ounces/
  ½ stick) butter or
  vegetable oil

Salt
Freshly ground black
  pepper

BOIL POTATOES in water to cover for 7 minutes or just until tender; drain well and set aside to cool. You may prepare the potatoes up to this point, cover, and refrigerate for several hours or overnight.

Melt butter or oil in large heavy cast-iron or nonstick skillet over medium-high heat. Add potatoes, sprinkle generously with salt and pepper, and cook for 10 minutes, turning occasionally and adding a little more butter if necessary (you shouldn't need more oil), or until potatoes are golden and crispy. Serves 4 to 6.

CAJUN HASH BROWNS

2 pounds (4 large) russet
   potatoes, peeled and cut
   into ¾-inch cubes
¼ cup vegetable oil
2 large garlic cloves,
   chopped
1 medium onion, chopped
1 large sweet red pepper,
   seeded and cut into
   1-inch pieces

1 teaspoon salt
½ teaspoon cayenne
1 teaspoon freshly ground
   black pepper
¼ teaspoon freshly ground
   white pepper
Several good dashes
   Tabasco sauce
4 large whole green onions,
   chopped

BOIL POTATOES in water to cover for 7 minutes or just until tender; drain well and set aside to cool. You may prepare the potatoes up to this point, cover, and refrigerate for several hours or overnight.

Heat oil in large heavy cast-iron or nonstick skillet over medium-high heat. Add potatoes, garlic, onion, red pepper, salt, cayenne, black pepper, white pepper, Tabasco sauce, and green onions and cook for 10 minutes, turning occasionally, or until potatoes are golden and crispy. Serves 6 to 8.

F*estive, spicy-hot, and hearty, this breakfast or lunch hash of chile-and-pepper-seasoned potatoes, onions, and sweet red pepper is utterly delightful.*

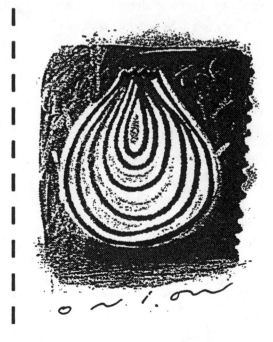

7 7

D rew and I love traveling by car and discovering taste treats along the way. Our philosophy is: if there isn't something yummy and unique to eat, then why go there?! A few years ago, we chanced upon the most delicious fries we'd ever eaten at a tavern in Reading, Pennsylvania. The secret – I realized after much pondering – was frying the potatoes in lard. ◆ Serve them the British way, with a generous sprinkling of malt vinegar and salt: I think you'll find them a delicious and welcome change from the standard American accompaniment – ketchup. ◆ I only serve these as an occasional treat now that lard is considered a sinful substance – but isn't everything these days?!

ULTIMATE FRENCH FRIES

1½ pounds (3 large) russet potatoes, scrubbed, unpeeled, and cut into ¼-inch strips

1 pound best-quality lard
Salt

AS POTATOES ARE SLICED, immediately drop them into a large bowl of ice water to help them stay crisp and white.

Heat lard in heavy, large, high-sided skillet or deep-fryer to 360°F.

Meanwhile, drain potatoes very well (they should not stay in the ice water any longer than it takes to finish cutting into strips). Lay strips in a single layer on clean dish towel, place another dish towel on top, and dry them completely.

In batches, and maintaining oil temperature at 360°F, fry strips just until they begin to color. Transfer potatoes, using a long-handled wire strainer or slotted spoon, to a footed wire strainer or basket set inside a bowl. (You may prepare the fries up to this point, a few hours before serving, then proceed with recipe.)

Just before serving, bring fat temperature back to 360°F and carefully return potatoes in one batch to oil. Cook for 2 minutes or until crisp and golden. Transfer potatoes, using a long-handled wire strainer or slotted spoon, to newspaper or brown paper grocery bag to drain (fries drained on paper towels won't remain crisp). Sprinkle with salt and serve at once. Serves 2 to 4.

EXCEPTIONAL FRENCH FRIES

2 pounds (4 large) russet potatoes, scrubbed, unpeeled, cut into ¼-inch strips

About 4 cups vegetable oil
Salt

AS POTATOES ARE SLICED, immediately drop them into a large bowl of ice water to help them stay crisp and white.

Heat 3 cups oil in heavy, large, high-sided skillet or deep-fryer to 360°F.

Meanwhile, drain potatoes very well (they should not stay in the ice water any longer than it takes to finish cutting into strips). Lay strips in a single layer on clean dish towel, place another dish towel on top, and dry them completely.

In batches, and maintaining oil temperature at 360°F, fry strips just until they begin to color. Transfer potatoes, using a long-handled wire strainer or slotted spoon, to a footed wire strainer or basket set inside a bowl.

Just before serving, add another cup of oil and bring temperature back to 360°F. Carefully return potatoes in one batch to oil. Cook for 2 minutes or until crisp and golden. Transfer potatoes, using a long-handled wire strainer or slotted spoon, to newspaper or brown paper grocery bag to drain. Sprinkle with salt and serve at once. Serves 4.

C*ooking the potatoes twice ensures perfectly crisp fries every time.* ♦ *Another secret to crispy fries is to drain them on newspaper or brown paper grocery bags – they steam and go soggy on paper towels. (I don't use a deep-fryer with a wire basket: I find the basket takes up too much space.)* ♦ *The first frying can be done a few hours ahead and the fries left in a wire basket or strainer. Then, just before serving, fry them again to sizzling crispness.* ♦ *For sweet potato fries, substitute sweet potatoes for the russets.*

F reshly-fried potato chips are unbelievably delicious. ◆ The potatoes must be sliced almost paper thin with a mandoline (a professional vegetable slicer). Available at restaurant supply shops, this wonderful tool is expensive, but worth every penny: it cuts perfectly uniform strips and slices every time. ◆ For sweet potato chips, simply substitute peeled sweet potatoes for the russets.

PERFECT POTATO CHIPS

2 pounds (4 large) russet potatoes, peeled or unpeeled, and very thinly sliced

4 cups vegetable oil
Salt

AS POTATOES ARE SLICED, immediately drop them into a large bowl of ice water to help them stay crisp and white.

Heat oil in heavy, large, high-sided skillet or deep-fryer to 360°F.

Meanwhile, drain potatoes very well (they should not stay in the ice water any longer than it takes to finish cutting into slices). Lay slices in a single layer on clean dish towel, place another dish towel on top, and dry them completely.

In batches, and maintaining oil temperature at 360°F, fry slices for 4 minutes or until golden brown. Transfer chips, using a long-handled wire strainer or slotted spoon, to newspaper or brown paper grocery bag to drain (chips drained on paper towels won't remain crisp). Sprinkle with salt and serve. Serves 4.

PARMESAN BASIL POTATO FRIES

1 pound (2 large) russet
  potatoes, scrubbed,
  unpeeled, and cut into
  ¼-inch strips
½ teaspoon salt
¼ teaspoon cayenne

1 tablespoon light olive oil
¼ cup freshly grated
  Parmesan cheese
2 tablespoons finely
  chopped fresh basil
  leaves

PREHEAT OVEN to 500°F.

Toss potatoes with salt and cayenne in medium bowl until thoroughly combined, then stir in oil to coat evenly.

Line baking sheet with foil and lightly oil. Arrange strips in single layer on prepared baking sheet. Bake for 15 minutes or until golden. Turn strips over and cook 5 minutes more or until fairly crisp and golden. (Don't overcook or the fries will be brittle instead of chewy-crisp.) Remove from oven, toss with cheese and basil, and transfer to serving dish. Serves 2.

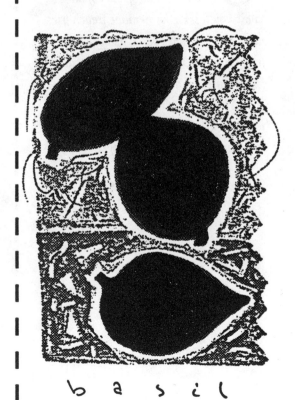

ven-baked fries are tossed in Parmesan cheese and ever so delicately scented with fresh basil.

basil

Once you try this healthy (and easy) version of french fries – "fried" in the oven using only 2 tablespoons of oil – I know you'll serve homemade french fries more often. Besides being healthier, the fries taste deliciously of potato instead of fat. ◆ I use a mandoline (a professional slicer) to cut the potatoes into perfect, uniform strips, but you may cut them by hand or use a french-fry gadget.

OVEN-BAKED FRENCH FRIES

2 pounds (4 large) russet potatoes, scrubbed, unpeeled, and cut into ¼-inch strips
4 cups cold water
2 tablespoons cider or malt vinegar
1½ teaspoons salt
2 tablespoons light olive or vegetable oil

AS POTATOES ARE SLICED, immediately drop them into a large bowl containing the cold water, vinegar, and ½ teaspoon salt; set aside for 30 minutes – no longer.

Preheat oven to 500°F.

Drain potatoes very well. Lay strips in a single layer on clean dish towel, place another dish towel on top, and dry them completely.

In clean, dry, large bowl, toss strips with remaining salt, then stir in oil to coat evenly.

Line 20- x 15-inch baking sheet (or 2 smaller sheets) with foil and lightly oil. Arrange strips in single layer on prepared baking sheet. Bake for 15 minutes or until golden on the underside, then turn strips over and cook 5 minutes more or until fairly crisp and golden. (Don't overcook or the fries will be brittle instead of chewy-crisp.) Transfer to large platter or individual dishes and serve at once with a sprinkling more salt if desired. Serves 2 to 4.

SPICY OVEN-BAKED FRENCH FRIES

2 pounds (4 large) russet
   potatoes, scrubbed,
   unpeeled, and cut into
   ¼-inch strips
4 cups cold water
2 tablespoons cider or
   malt vinegar

1½ teaspoons salt
2 teaspoons chili powder
1 teaspoon paprika
2 tablespoons light olive or
   vegetable oil

AS POTATOES ARE SLICED, immediately drop them into a large bowl containing the cold water, vinegar, and ½ teaspoon salt; set aside to soak for 30 minutes – no longer.

Preheat oven to 500°F.

Drain potatoes very well. Lay strips in a single layer on clean dish towel, place another dish towel on top, and dry them completely.

In clean, dry, large bowl, toss strips with remaining salt, chili powder, and paprika until thoroughly combined, then stir in oil to coat evenly.

Line 20- x 15-inch baking sheet (or 2 smaller sheets) with foil and lightly oil. Arrange strips in single layer on prepared baking sheet. Bake for 15 minutes or until golden on the underside, then turn strips over and cook 5 minutes more or until fairly crisp and golden. (Don't overcook or the fries will be brittle instead of chewy-crisp.) Transfer to a large platter or individual dishes and serve at once with a sprinkling more salt if desired. Serves 2 to 4.

I n this spicy version of Oven-Baked French Fries, the potato strips are enlivened with the bite of chili powder and paprika.

Beta-blast fresh fries – what a great way to get your daily dose of beta-carotene! ◆ The only difficulty is cutting the sweet potatoes – they're more dense than white potatoes – so do use a heavy, very sharp knife. ◆ You'll love the flavor and the chewy texture of these wonderful fries.

OVEN-BAKED SWEET-POTATO FRIES

1 pound (2 medium-large) sweet potatoes, peeled and cut lengthwise into ½-inch thick wedges	2 teaspoons vegetable oil 1 teaspoon salt

PREHEAT OVEN to 450°F.

Toss potatoes with oil and salt in large bowl until coated evenly.

Line 12- x 17-inch baking sheet with foil and lightly oil. Arrange wedges in single layer on prepared baking sheet Bake for 20 minutes or until tender and chewy-crisp; don't overcook. Transfer to platter and serve at once with a sprinkling more salt if desired. Serves 2.

BREADS

♦ ♦ ♦

V*ibrantly-colored, lightly-crunchy muffins with a healthy dose of vitamins and fiber – what more can you ask of a muffin?*

SWEET POTATO CORNMEAL MUFFINS

1 pound (2 medium-large) sweet potatoes
1 cup all-purpose flour
1 cup yellow cornmeal
1 tablespoon baking powder
2 tablespoons sugar
¾ teaspoon salt
½ teaspoon baking soda
1 cup buttermilk
2 large eggs
2 tablespoons melted butter

PREHEAT OVEN to 400°F.

Bake potatoes for 1 hour or until tender; scoop out flesh, mash until smooth, and set aside to cool.

Adjust oven rack to top third position. Coat 12-cup muffin pan with vegetable spray.

Using a whisk, thoroughly mix flour, cornmeal, baking powder, sugar, salt, and baking soda in large bowl. In medium bowl, whisk buttermilk, eggs, butter, and sweet potatoes until completely combined. Pour liquid ingredients over dry ingredients and fold in with rubber spatula *just* until combined; do not overmix.

Spoon batter into prepared muffin cups, dividing it evenly. Bake for 20 minutes or until tester comes out clean. Turn out onto rack and serve warm or at room temperature. Makes 12 muffins.

POPPY SEED POTATO ROLLS

1 envelope dry yeast
1 cup milk, scalded and
  cooled to lukewarm
½ cup sugar
½ cup warm unseasoned
  mashed potatoes
  (1 medium russet)
½ cup (4 ounces/1 stick)
  butter, melted

2 teaspoons salt
2 large eggs, lightly beaten
About 4¼ cups all-purpose
  flour
2 tablespoons melted butter
1½ tablespoons poppy
  seeds

IN LARGE BOWL combine yeast with milk and sugar; set aside for 10 minutes or until foamy.

Stir in mashed potatoes, ½ cup butter, salt, and eggs until thoroughly blended.

Stir in 3 cups flour until combined, then knead in another cup flour. Turn out onto floured surface and knead in only enough flour to form a soft dough. Continue kneading for 5 minutes or until smooth. Place dough in a clean, lightly greased large bowl and cover with plastic wrap; set aside for 1½ hours or until doubled in bulk.

Gently punch down dough, remove to lightly floured surface, and roll to 1-inch thick rectangle. Cut dough into 2½-inch squares and arrange in greased 9 x 13-inch baking pan, barely touching each other. Brush tops with melted butter, sprinkle with poppy seeds, cover with plastic wrap, and let rise for 25 minutes or until almost doubled.

Preheat oven to 400°F. Bake for 20 to 30 minutes or until golden brown and cooked through. Serve warm. Makes about 16 rolls.

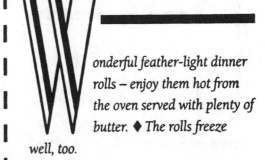

onderful feather-light dinner rolls – enjoy them hot from the oven served with plenty of butter. ◆ *The rolls freeze well, too.*

Chewy-textured bread with a wonderful flavor redolent of English muffins. ♦ Use the second-largest openings of a 4-sided grater to grate the potato. ♦ You may freeze the cooled bread – either sliced or unsliced – if wrapped completely in foil and placed in a freezer bag. To thaw, place foil-wrapped bread in a preheated 350°F oven and heat until completely warmed through.

POTATO BREAD

1 envelope dry yeast
1 cup lukewarm water
¼ teaspoon sugar
1 teaspoon salt

¾ cup finely grated peeled russet potato including liquid exuded (about 2 medium)
About 3 cups unbleached all-purpose flour

PUT YEAST, water, and sugar into bowl of heavy-duty mixer or large mixing bowl; stir and set aside for 10 minutes or until foamy. Stir in salt and grated potato.

Add 3 cups flour to bowl and either beat using dough hook or knead by hand, adding more flour only if necessary to make a soft, somewhat sticky dough. Beat for 3 minutes, or knead by hand for 10 minutes, until dough becomes smooth and satiny.

Lightly oil large clean bowl and place dough in bowl. Cover bowl tightly with plastic wrap to ensure dough doesn't form a crust. Set aside for 2 hours or until tripled in bulk. (You can let the dough rise several hours at room temperature, or overnight in refrigerator if desired.)

Punch dough down and transfer to generously floured surface. Cut dough in half to form two loaves. Roll each one into 11-inch cylinder shape while rolling in flour to completely – but lightly – cover surface. Twist each loaf two half turns to form creases. Place loaves on lightly floured baking sheet, cover with clean dish towel, and let rise 30 minutes.

Meanwhile, preheat oven to 350°F. Bake loaves for 25 minutes or until pale golden color and loaves sound hollow when tapped on the bottom; don't overcook. Transfer to rack and cover bread with clean dish towel to soften crust while cooling. Serve warm. Makes 2 loaves.

DESSERTS

◆ ◆ ◆

C ountry cooks from times past began adding mashed potatoes to all manner of baked goods to help them stay fresh and moist. ♦ In warm weather it's best to refrigerate the cake to keep the frosting from softening, but bring to room temperature before serving.

CHOCOLATE POTATO CAKE

¾ cup unsweetened cocoa
    powder
2 cups all-purpose flour
1 teaspoon baking powder
1 teaspoon baking soda
½ teaspoon salt
1 teaspoon ground
    cinnamon
1 teaspoon powdered
    instant coffee
1 cup (8 ounces/2 sticks)
    butter, at room
    temperature
2 cups sugar
4 large eggs
1 teaspoon vanilla

1 cup unseasoned mashed
    potatoes, cooled
    (1 large russet)
1 cup buttermilk
FROSTING
3 cups confectioners' sugar
¼ cup unsweetened cocoa
    powder
⅛ teaspoon salt
½ cup (4 ounces/1 stick)
    butter, at room
    temperature
¼ cup sour cream
1 teaspoon vanilla
1 tablespoon grated
    orange zest

SIFT TOGETHER cocoa, flour, baking powder, baking soda, salt, cinnamon, and coffee in medium bowl.

Cream butter and sugar in large bowl of electric mixer for 3 minutes or until light and fluffy. Beat in eggs one at a time, then vanilla and mashed potatoes. On low spread, beat in dry ingredients alternately with buttermilk just until blended. Pour batter into two greased and floured 9-inch round baking pans. Bake in preheated 350°F oven for 30 minutes or until tester comes out clean when inserted into center; don't overcook. Cool in pans, then prepare frosting.

Thoroughly blend all frosting ingredients in food processor until smooth. Spread between cake layers and on top and sides of cooled cake. Makes 1 cake.

SWEET POTATO PIE IN
CHOCOLATE CRUMB CRUST

2 pounds (4 medium-large) sweet potatoes	2 large eggs
1½ cups chocolate wafer cookie crumbs (about 8 ounces cookies)	1 teaspoon vanilla
	¼ teaspoon salt
	½ teaspoon ground cinnamon
6 tablespoons butter, melted	¼ teaspoon grated nutmeg
¾ cup sugar	¼ teaspoon ground allspice
½ cup (4 ounces/1 stick) butter	Finely grated zest 1 medium lemon

BAKE POTATOES in a preheated 425°F oven for 1 hour or until tender.

Meanwhile, blend crumbs with melted butter and pat into bottom and up sides of 9-inch pie plate; set aside.

When potatoes are tender, mash flesh with potato masher in large bowl and set aside to cool to room temperature.

Reduce oven heat to 350°F and bake cookie crust for 8 minutes; return heat to 400°F.

Whisk potatoes, sugar, ½ cup butter, eggs, vanilla, salt, cinnamon, nutmeg, allspice, and lemon zest until thoroughly combined. Pour into pie crust and bake for 1 hour or until tester inserted into center comes out clean. Allow to cool completely, then chill thoroughly before slicing. Makes 1 pie.

I just love the look – and taste – of this bright-orange, smooth-textured filling set in a dark chocolate cookie-crumb crust. It looks simply superb when sliced in small wedges and topped with a scoop of vanilla ice cream or whipped cream.
♦ Keep the pie refrigerated until serving.

I found this recipe in an old cookbooklet from the '40s. These moist cookies have the taste and texture of chocolate cake, so why not gild the lily and spread them with your favorite chocolate frosting?

CHOCOLATE POTATO DROP COOKIES

½ cup (4 ounces) vegetable shortening
1 cup packed brown sugar
1 large egg
1 teaspoon vanilla
2 squares unsweetened chocolate, melted and cooled

½ cup unseasoned mashed potatoes (about 1 medium russet), cooled
1½ cups all-purpose flour
½ teaspoon salt
½ teaspoon baking soda
¾ cup buttermilk
1 cup currants

CREAM SHORTENING and sugar in large bowl of electric mixer for 3 minutes or until light and fluffy. Beat in egg, vanilla, chocolate, and potatoes until well combined.

Whisk flour, salt, and baking soda in medium bowl until blended.

On low speed, blend in flour mixture and buttermilk alternately until smooth. Stir in currants.

Drop by rounded tablespoons onto greased baking sheet. Bake in preheated 400°F oven for 10 minutes or until cookies spring back when pressed with finger; don't overcook. Transfer to rack and cool before serving. Makes 3½ dozen.

INDEX

INDEX